PORTRAIT OF A WOMAN

by
MICHEL VINAVER

Translation from the French
by
DONALD WATSON

The Dramatic Publishing Company
Woodstock, Illinois • London, England • Melbourne, Australia

PORTRAIT OF A WOMAN

A Full Length Play
For Eleven Actors

CHARACTERS

SOPHIE AUZANNEAU ⎫
XAVIER BERGERET ⎪
CORNAILLE ⎬ medical students
LACHAUD ⎪
CLAUDETTE ⎭

COLONNA ...on the teaching staff of the Faculty of Medicine
MONSIEUR AUZANNEAU ....Sophie's father
MADAME AUZANNEAU ....Sophie's mother
MADAME GUIBOT .... Sophie's landlady
DR. BERND SCHLESSINGER ....surgeon
GERBIER .... gunsmith
FRANCINE .... Xavier Bergeret's fiancée
THE PRESIDENT ...... of the Court of Assizes in Paris
THE PUBLIC PROSECUTOR
MAÎTRE LUBET .... Counsel for the plaintiff
MAÎTRE CANCÉ ....Counsel for the defence
DR. HAUDEBOURG ....expert

The following parts are played by one performer:
   M. AUZANNEAU, GERBIER, DR. SCHLESSINGER
   MME. AUZANNEAU, MME. GUIBOT
   LACHAUD, DR. HAUDEBOURG
   CORNAILLE, COLONNA
   FRANCINE, CLAUDETTE

Eleven actors take seventeen parts. The changes of appearance (costume, hairpieces, etc.) needed for the five actors playing more than one role are made swiftly and perfunctorily in full view of the audience.

The play is continuous
and is performed without an interval.

ABOUT THE SETTING

A circular or oval stage with no fixed decor. A stagehand, in constant attendance, is ready as the action unfolds to introduce, remove or change round the portable items of the setting. These are of two strongly contrasted types. On the one hand the chairs, tables, beds, doors, etc., belonging to the outside world...monochrome, undifferentiated, inexpressive and interchangeable, blending together to serve various functions, brought on or taken off only as the need arises. On the other hand the ultra-realistic representation of the Court of Assizes in Paris in 1953; or rather a fragmentary suggestion of it, isolated pieces of an unfinished jigsaw puzzle, each one executed in *trompe-l'oeil.* Human figures can be represented in these items (assessors, clerk of the court, guards, jurymen, photographers, journalists, the general public), which never leave the stage though they are subject to continual rearrangement, by sudden changes or by smooth transition, to create an impression of constant movement. A soundtrack intermittently reproduces the mutterings, laughter, exclamations and disruptions from the public.

PORTRAIT OF A WOMAN

AT RISE: *The STAGEHAND appears, brings on a landing door and installs it in the centre of the stage. On one side of the door is the staircase of an apartment block; on the other, where the STAGEHAND places a chair and an armchair on either side of a table, is Xavier's bedsitter, 25 rue de l'Abbé Groult, Paris XV, on the seventh floor. XAVIER comes and sits in the armchair. Pause. SOPHIE appears on the landing.*

PRESIDENT. She walked up to the seventh floor
Why didn't you use the lift?

MME. GUIBOT. Forewarned is forearmed
What's more the boy was warned twice two telegrams the same day one from me and one from his dad

PRESIDENT. Your telegram despatched from Lillle on the 15th of March was couched in the following terms "Sophie gone to Paris stop avoid meeting urgent"

MME. GUIBOT. Better safe than sorry Mr. President so I warned his dad as well

PRESIDENT. And the same day the father sent the following telegram to his son "return immediately Saint-Omer"

(SOPHIE rings at the door. XAVIER waits for a time, stands up, moves to the door, hesitates, then opens it. SOPHIE enters the room.)

5

XAVIER. What are you doing here?

SOPHIE. I had to see you *(SOPHIE moves quickly forward and sits on the chair. XAVIER returns to his armchair.)*

XAVIER. I told you we shouldn't see each other any more

PRESIDENT. Several remarks were exchanged more or less in the same vein

SOPHIE. I couldn't not see you again things I've got to explain

XAVIER. There's nothing left for us to say you know

SOPHIE. I can't help it you've got to hear me out
Listen

XAVIER. What difference will it make?

SOPHIE. I can't

XAVIER. Listen Sophie that's the way it is

SOPHIE. What way?

XAVIER. It's all over *(SOPHIE takes a revolver from her raincoat pocket and fires to hit him in the forehead. XAVIER collapses over the table. She stands up and shoots him in the back. Then she fires a third time, into his ear.)*

SOPHIE. I walked up to the seventh floor because I needed time to think out what I had to tell him find the right words to use I hoped if I knew how to talk to him I could make him feel sorry and win him over

PRESIDENT. And failing that put an end to him and then commit suicide?

(She nods her head slowly in confirmation.)

Only you forgot

In your disturbed state

To turn the weapon on yourself

MAÎTRE LUBET. Understandably Monsieur le President what else can one expect? In the heat of the moment one can't think of everything

SOPHIE. Face to face I couldn't say any of the things I wanted to

He seemed so distant

Almost a stranger

LUBET. So you might as well have taken the lift

SOPHIE. It happened so quickly

It was over before I realised

I was so worked up

PRESIDENT. You know how to fire a gun

One bullet at zero range the other two point-blank

PUBLIC PROSECUTOR. Yes he collapses the first time you fire but do you then put your arm around him and cry "Xavier speak to me what have I done?"

No you aim a second shot into his back do your nerves get the better of you?

No you fire a final bullet at zero range into his ear

And this Sophie Auzanneau and I'm appalled to have to say it to a young girl like you

This is what you did and didn't do

LUBET. How did you deliver the fatal shot? What position was he in? Head slumped over like this? Or like this?

SOPHIE. I can't give you the details sir if I could remember I'd tell you

LUBET. Hm and after that?

You were found on the kitchen floor with the gas turned on

Oh yes a revolver's too brutal you prefer gas you know all about that from your medical studies that there's not so much risk lying flat on the floor and you hadn't forgotten

MAÎTRE CANCÉ. I deny the implication that between the three shots there was breathing space to think

That was a mean suggestion

Cheap and cruel

It was murder that's true she meant to kill and she did isn't that enough for you?

No you have to turn it into a novelette distort the facts and serve them up like a fisherman's yarn

MME. GUIBOT. Still he had been warned

PRESIDENT. Forewarned as he was how do you explain that he opened the door?

MME. GUIBOT. He was a young gentleman none better nice as they come

Well brought up good manners

PRESIDENT. He knew he was at risk

LACHAUD. He was on his guard but perhaps deep down he wasn't

He passed the telegram on to me and said "here take it if anything happens to me you can prove there was malice aforethought" but whether he believed it or not

PRESIDENT. He didn't follow his father's advice which reads more like an order "return immediately Saint-Omer"

LACHAUD. Xavier was anything but chicken

CORNAILLE. But those telegrams were on his mind he spent the last two days of his life rather like someone on the run

LACHAUD. He stuck close to his friends either sleeping at their place or persuading them to come to his

CORNAILLE. She managed to catch up with him she wanted to see him tête-à-tête he put the meeting off

made a date in the Place de l'Odéon for the 17th at
9:45

PRESIDENT. But persistent as she was she posted herself
the previous evening in a café opposite No. 25 rue de
l'Abbé Groult

PUBLIC PROSECUTOR. Sees him come home walks up
to his apartment with the revolver in her coat pocket

PRESIDENT. Sophie Auzanneau after you recovered con-
sciousness when the police questioned you you de-
clared "all I know is I took my revolver out to kill myself in front of Xavier but I can't remember anything
that happened from the moment the first shot went off"
Do you still stick to this version of the facts?

SOPHIE. No

PRESIDENT. And what is today's version?

SOPHIE. It's not a version, sir
I wanted to kill us both yes at the time I mean to bring
him down with me both of us together

LUBET. You no longer maintain you killed Bergeret by
accident?

SOPHIE. No

LUBET. So you lied to the police?

SOPHIE. Yes

LUBET. Yet today you're indignant if we cast doubt on a
single word you say, on this matter Monsieur le
Président

SOPHIE. Sir I have nothing more to add

LUBET. Except that in your shoes Sophie Auzanneau I'd
show a little less indignation and a great deal more remorse

SOPHIE. You're not in my shoes

LUBET. For you will have noticed Ladies and Gentlemen
of the Jury that nothing the defendant has said so far

CANCÉ. I protest Monsieur le Président
LUBET. Betrays the slightest trace of remorse
PRESIDENT. I must have order in the Court
    I will not hesitate if the need arises to suspend this
    hearing
    I will ensure come what may that these proceedings be
    conducted in an orderly manner
    I ask the defendant

(The terrace of a café in Lille.)

SOPHIE. Me? What do I like? To be always changing
    new situations like a boy following you when a
    lecture's over
XAVIER. That's not very new
    There aren't hundreds of new situations
    You can count them on the fingers of one hand three or
    four at the most
    Each with a number of variations
SOPHIE. The number of situations is infinite
    And each time the world begins again
XAVIER. A world like that would be unthinkable
SOPHIE. What good does thinking do?
XAVIER. To grasp things
SOPHIE. To let them grasp you
XAVIER. To be passive?
SOPHIE. To drift
XAVIER. Anywhere?
SOPHIE. Wherever
XAVIER. That's what you believe?
SOPHIE. Chance and fate are two sides of the same coin
XAVIER. I believe one can and should take control of
    one's life

SOPHIE. What for?

XAVIER. To get somewhere

SOPHIE. Are you serious?

XAVIER. I don't mean a career or happiness maybe what
  I mean is the image you have of yourself

SOPHIE. My elder brother was drowned in his submarine
  The younger one died in his fighter plane a few months
  later on an exercise it crashed

XAVIER. What's that got to do with it?

SOPHIE. There's such a gap between us

XAVIER. Perhaps that's why I wanted to follow you

SOPHIE. What about cats? Do you like black cats? A
  black cat stalking through the long grass?

XAVIER. Where are you from? If you don't mind my
  asking?

SOPHIE. My family live in the suburbs of Dunkirk I was
  born in Dunkirk a town that was a fort

  Inert they talk about the force of inertia don't they?

  You've very polite

  Do you like long beaches?

  I love pebbles all kinds of stones

  I pick them up fill my pockets with them

  I'd like to break them open to see what's inside

XAVIER. Shall we have supper together this evening?

SOPHIE. Do I interest you? I must find out about you
  what you like. I bet you love kicking a ball about you
  look like a striker you do play football? Where's your
  family from?

XAVIER. My father's a vet at Arras

  I'm not a bad cook you can come to my place

SOPHIE. All the boys I meet want to cook for me

  It's a stroke of luck because I

  But I've got some revision to do

XAVIER. We'll revise together

SOPHIE. Will you ask me some stinkers about the cervical vertebrae?

XAVIER. Or the iliac bone

SOPHIE. It's such a huge subject

XAVIER. Colonna does his best to make a shambles of it

SOPHIE. Oh him and his urinary tract he's fanatical about it
The urethra I ask you and the bladder what a bore I easily get swamped

XAVIER. All depends on the prof
Colonna's hard to follow
I'll grill you some sardines

SOPHIE. I hate sardines
Specially oven-grilled with mustard my mother's favourite dish the smell lingers in the house all year round

(At the Auzanneaus' house in the suburbs of Dunkirk.)

MME. AUZANNEAU. That storm's played havoc with the garden

SOPHIE. It doesn't really matter you know

MME. AUZANNEAU. Reminds me of the storm we had when our little girl left home and we only found out later she'd gone to the hospital to become a nurse

XAVIER. You're on bad terms with her?

SOPHIE. This all sounds like the start of a novel

M. AUZANNEAU. And a tart

MME. AUZANNEAU. How do we know what went on?
She wasn't even seventeen and he was at least fifty-five

M. AUZANNEAU. What are we eating?

MME. AUZANNEAU. A nice tail-end of cod
Fresh from market this morning.

At least that Schlessinger was a decent sort of chap
who made sure she had proper meals

(In a bar in Paris.)

FRANCINE. I've been so scared
MME. AUZANNEAU. She hadn't even stopped growing
M. AUZANNEAU. A disaster for the beans
MME. AUZANNEAU. And those hailstones
　　The tomatoes all peppered with them
FRANCINE. You you're always so punctual
　　Oh Xavier I imagined all sorts of things
　　I thought she must have tracked you down
M. AUZANNEAU. She was sixteen when she took off
　　and that was the start because you put up with all her
　　shenanigans
　　I must go and prop up that pear tree

(At GERBIER's [the gunsmith] in Lille.)

SOPHIE. How much is that one?
MME. AUZANNEAU. It would be the one with the best
　　pears
　　But she'll settle down again
　　It's the times we live in
　　The war
SOPHIE. And that one?
　　I know nothing about them you know
　　To fire it
GERBIER. First you load it
SOPHIE. Yes of course you load it
XAVIER. Poor darling
　　But I don't want to keep you in the dark

She found me and I'm sure it wasn't by accident she
knew my movements

It's hopeless you get the feeling you can't get through
to her with words

FRANCINE. And then? After that?

XAVIER. I told her about you and me

GERBIER. Take a good look

FRANCINE. When you're jealous you don't listen

XAVIER. To be jealous you have to be in love she
doesn't love me

FRANCINE. I'm not so sure all I know is that you don't
love her because you love me

You do love me?

XAVIER. Sure as this table's a table

FRANCINE. Fancy comparing

XAVIER. I'm not comparing you to the table

FRANCINE. You're comparing our love to a table

SOPHIE. And what does one do next?

XAVIER. All I mean is our love is as real as this table
My love

FRANCINE. I thought it was stronger than that
Never mind what did she want?

GERBIER. That's it then you take aim

SOPHIE. Nothing too complicated

GERBIER. What matters is how you look after it
If you want it to give you good service
You make a weapon last by taking good care of it
This pistol here see made in 1780 it's always been in
the Bonachon family we've been gunsmiths since 1720

SOPHIE. Are you a Bonachon?

GERBIER. Yes and no I married a Bonachon
My name's Gerbier but Bonachon's still the firm's name
You've got a licence?

SOPHIE. You need a licence?

GERBIER. I'd advise you to choose this one
It's easier to handle

MME. GUIBOT. She showed me her revolver sir oh she
never kept nothing from me not a bit sly no almost the
opposite

PRESIDENT. Meaning what?

MME. GUIBOT. If she had a bee in her bonnet she went
overboard

PRESIDENT. But she didn't go over the top for this boy

MME. GUIBOT. Not to start with

PRESIDENT. At the start it was Bergeret who was mad
about her

MME. GUIBOT. Yes

LUBET. The fact that she wasn't so keen on Bergeret
Didn't stop her slipping between his sheets
But she didn't mind changing her sheets did she?
It's even said she could do without sheets
The oilcloth on a kitchen table would do

PRESIDENT. Order

LUBET. I have here a letter addressed to her by one of
her former lovers in which allusion is clearly made to
the corner of a kitchen table covered with a pink and
white oilcloth

CANCÉ. All is grist to my learned friend's mill even if he
risks contradicting his own argument
If there had been intent wouldn't my client have taken
care before committing the crime to destroy this inti-
mate correspondence the contents of which could
clearly be used against her?
The bare facts speak for themselves but you no you
have to spice them up and so mask their authentic fla-
vour

Too spicy by half

It's unfair to single out one sentence

What I want you to arrive at Members of the Jury is a total view of a complex human being of a whole live person who merits your understanding however guilty she may be but you must remain cool and curb your abhorrence if you are to listen attentively to the innermost promptings of her heart

Hard as it is for you to enter this emotional arena here alone is there a chance some answer may emerge to the fearful question you have to resolve

Why did she do it?

LUBET. Self-interest as I shall demonstrate

For want of any argument he can get his teeth in my esteemed colleague is riding a fashionable hobby-horse in-depth psychology which as we know will permit him to make any claim he likes even to call a black cat white. Why do I speak of a black cat? We have evidence according to which the defendant had a passion for a black cat

No doubt her one and only genuine passion

But apart from that my learned friend we know how predisposed you are to dredge everything up from the vertiginous depths of the soul

Petty of me perhaps but I'm concerned with the facts

I stick to the facts

(SOPHIE's room in Lille.)

MME. GUIBOT. Like the butcher f'r instance he's all upset waiting for his bill to be paid

'Course *I* don't complain about you only you owe me the last two months' rent

My sunniest room I only have one per floor with two
windows and you've got the top one looks over the
trees

The one everyone asks for

You must say if you want to stay

XAVIER. She threatened to kill me I mean she made a
scene

MME. GUIBOT. If you're staying it's all right by me

FRANCINE. Did you love her very much?

MME. GUIBOT. I've got used to you

XAVIER. For me she was a demon

MME. GUIBOT. Even if you've got lots of things on your
mind and not all of them nice ones

You mustn't forget to pay me

FRANCINE. More than me? Did you love her more than
me?

MME. GUIBOT. If you're staying

You're always tearing from place to place

XAVIER. It hurts me that love can come to an end

MME. GUIBOT. No good tormenting yourself like this

FRANCINE. Hers?

XAVIER. Mine

'Cos she never loved *me*

MME. GUIBOT. You ought to empty your head of this
rubbish for good an' all

XAVIER. When I broke with her she was annoyed not
upset

That's what my friends told me

FRANCINE. One day you might stop loving me too?

XAVIER. With those big round glasses of yours

My sweet angel

FRANCINE. Aren't you scared?

XAVIER. You know I'm not

I ought to be

Cornaille thinks if I don't clear off abroad for six months without leaving an address

SOPHIE. No I can't marry you

XAVIER. Why?

SOPHIE. Deep down I'm sure of it you you're so positive

XAVIER. So what?

SOPHIE. So stable so clear

I'm staying Madame Guibot I'm staying

MME. GUIBOT. Just as well just as well you're in no state too much running through that head of yours and you can't go on like this on an empty stomach

Two days you've gone without food

XAVIER. I try to reason myself into being scared

MME. GUIBOT. You must eat

SOPHIE. I can't

XAVIER. But you know

MME. GUIBOT. A cup of tea and some chocolate biscuits I bought you

XAVIER. It's my weakness I believe everyone is naturally good

SOPHIE. I can't marry you

FRANCINE. Go away if you have to

Don't give your address even to me not to anyone I'll wait a year for you two years

XAVIER. It was Lachaud slipped her my address

She was waiting for me outside the Faculty she'd checked up she knew what time I came out

MME. GUIBOT. For two days now you've been shut in your room

Curled up in a ball on your bed

FRANCINE. Xavier oh Xavier listen

All sorts of ideas are rushing through my mind

MME. GUIBOT. Shut him out of your heart Mademoiselle Sophie once and for all if you'll take my advice

SOPHIE. I can't

MME. GUIBOT. And in three or six months you'll see you'll be a different person

SOPHIE. He's dug his claws into me

FRANCINE. When you come back we'll open your surgery can you see me in a white coat? I'll note down your appointments you'd like me to be your assistant? At the start we'll be living from hand to mouth but then

SOPHIE. I feel as if I'm sinking

FRANCINE. You'll see and even

When we've had time to build up a practice

MME. GUIBOT. You like them these little biscuits? Come on it'll all work out in time

SOPHIE. I can't hang on any longer I'll end up doing something dreadful

MME. GUIBOT. That's what she said

SOPHIE. I don't care if I'm not a good loser I don't love him enough to watch him walk off with somebody else

MME. GUIBOT. And she showed me her gun she held out her arm

CANCÉ. Do you think of her as a cold-blooded criminal?

MME. GUIBOT. And she went and took it from under her pillow

And brandished it in my face and she told me

If you want my opinion she's not all there maybe she does put on an act but she gets too caught up in the part she's playing and then she overdoes it

SOPHIE. What fate decrees that must we blindly obey

(At the Auzanneaus' in Dunkirk.)

MME. AUZANNEAU. It's no use
　　Your answer's always the same
CANCÉ. She's meant to be hard-hearted
M. AUZANNEAU. Because it's always the same old story
MME. AUZANNEAU. When we first met it wasn't like
　　this
CANCÉ. But underneath the armour she's built up
M. AUZANNEAU. It was exactly the same
MME. AUZANNEAU. You saw me in a different light
　　It's no use
CANCÉ. A poor heart was desperately beating
M. AUZANNEAU. If we've got to go back that far
　　I saw you as the sweet little darling you were
MME. AUZANNEAU. Like the sweet little darlings you
　　ogle today when they walk past under the window
CANCÉ. Locked away in prison
M. AUZANNEAU. Haven't you done enough nagging?
　　What is it you want?
　　For us to go out dancing? We'll do some jiving
　　Ha ha ha
　　Tomorrow for our little girl's birthday
　　Any of that stew left over?
　　You ought to give us sardines
　　It's a long time
MME. AUZANNEAU. Tomorrow
M. AUZANNEAU. Our little girl loves them
MME. AUZANNEAU. What about the present?
M. AUZANNEAU. How many years has she been telling
　　us not to put ourselves out for her?
MME. AUZANNEAU. It's true with her we could never
　　get it right

M. AUZANNEAU. What we did last year three thousand francs in an envelope she never turns her nose up at that

MME. AUZANNEAU. This year Louis you could make it five thousand everything's so expensive

(At GERBIER's in Lille.)

SOPHIE. How much does it cost?

MME. AUZANNEAU. It's her brothers she's missing you know

GERBIER. Four thousand eight hundred

SOPHIE. Oh I've not got enough

(A bistro in Lille.)

CORNAILLE. Cut your losses

LACHAUD. The bloody fool's blubbing

GERBIER. How much have you got without indiscretion?

SOPHIE. Two thousand five hundred

GERBIER. If you cross the road there's a toyshop where they sell water-pistols

CORNAILLE. What good does crying do? Belt her one
Take your choice either you belt her give her a beating she won't forget or you say cheerio hello and goodbye Sophie best of luck with Colonna

LACHAUD. Give her the push

XAVIER. But I'm crazy about her

CORNAILLE. A damn good hiding then
Because she's taking you for a ride

PRESIDENT. So it was then you set your cap at Xavier Bergeret
A decent young man clever and ambitious

From a close-knit family well regarded in Saint Omer
Answer me

SOPHIE. Yes Monsieur le Président

LACHAUD. The way she flaunts herself

CORNAILLE. The three of us'll gang up and bash her about

LACHAUD. Like a tart

PRESIDENT. His father was a vet a man of means

LACHAUD. Beat her up

CORNAILLE. If you let it drag on

PRESIDENT. A good choice
A comfortable prospect for you gilt-edged no?

SOPHIE. Yes Monsieur le Président

LACHAUD. She plays the field to get up your nose

CORNAILLE. It's not Colonna she's after
What she wants is to watch you getting all screwed up
while she makes a play for Colonna

PRESIDENT. In other words you had everything to make you happy

LACHAUD. For the whole world to see

SOPHIE. I don't know

PRESIDENT. Nor presumably do you know the reason why
When you had found someone to love you
You gave in to this Monsieur Colonna?

LACHAUD. That's the way she loves you

CORNAILLE. She'll be the death of you

LACHAUD. Stop being a bloody fool Xavier

XAVIER. It would be easy if she was only aiming this at me
For some reason I don't understand she's doing it
To hurt herself

SOPHIE. I don't know

CORNAILLE. A good hiding

XAVIER. I don't think

CORNAILLE. That's what she's asking for

PRESIDENT. You don't know?
 Let's say it's a classic ploy for a woman
 Jealousy fans the flame you can find examples of it in
 all the best authors can't you?

XAVIER. To drift

SOPHIE. I don't know

PRESIDENT. But you've told us you devoured all kinds
 of novels perched up there in your pear tree

XAVIER. The first time I met her she told me that's what
 she liked to drift

LACHAUD. What she needed as a kid was
 A proper dad
 I'm not sure but you can imagine
 If he'd given her the odd spanking she was after

(At the Auzanneaus' in Dunkirk.)

MME. AUZANNEAU. You look peaky Sophie
 You getting enough to eat?

LACHAUD. That's what she wants from you

CORNAILLE. She's dying for it

MME. AUZANNEAU. Since last year you've lost weight
 But as we only see you on your birthday

M. AUZANNEAU. You tell her that every time

MME. AUZANNEAU. You don't take enough care of
 yourself

M. AUZANNEAU. Off we go again

MME. AUZANNEAU. What?

M. AUZANNEAU. It's no use

SOPHIE. I've been working hard Mum

MME. AUZANNEAU. If we saw a little more of you

SOPHIE. I paid you a visit in September did you forget?

MME. AUZANNEAU. A flying visit

XAVIER. It's not in my nature

SOPHIE. To pick up my winter things

LACHAUD. Later will be too late

CORNAILLE. It's now or never

XAVIER. The moment's neither here nor there it's not like that with her

MME. AUZANNEAU. You don't look well

Do you get enough sleep?

You should come and spend part of the summer here to build yourself up again

LACHAUD. The shrew's asking to be tamed

SOPHIE. They failed me in my exam

CORNAILLE. Tame her or chuck her out

M. AUZANNEAU. And you say you've been working?

SOPHIE. Looks as if you've redone the roof

XAVIER. Sophie's beautiful inside and out

M. AUZANNEAU. The gale blew half of it away

XAVIER. She's fighting against God knows what

M. AUZANNEAU. Nothing left of the beans

The pear tree

MME. AUZANNEAU. And the tomatoes

XAVIER. Struggling against something inside her that's breaking her up

M. AUZANNEAU. The storm split the pear tree in two

XAVIER. It's got nothing to do with her nature

Sophie's not a nympho she hasn't got it in her

SOPHIE. My pear tree?

M. AUZANNEAU. To say nothing about the others

CORNAILLE. You must snap out of your dreamworld

MME. AUZANNEAU. And you're still seeing that boy?

LACHAUD. She's screwing with Colonna

SOPHIE. Xavier he got through

CORNAILLE. Colonna's a better bet than you are

SOPHIE. I'm sitting it again next session

In the spring we're getting married setting up in Paris
Doctor Xavier and Doctor Sophie Bergeret
Sound good?

I want to go and see the pear tree
You didn't cut it down?

MME. AUZANNEAU. Well say something why don't you tell her?

Dad managed to save it the trunk was split all the way down he put a clamp round it

M. AUZANNEAU. We'll have to wait till spring

MME. AUZANNEAU. Give her the envelope
Oh Louis why don't you tell her for once?
For your twenty-fourth birthday here's an envelope you really deserve it because you've worked hard

M. AUZANNEAU. So hard they failed her
Ha ha ha

MME. AUZANNEAU. Don't pay attention to your father's little jokes you know him and if you get married

There'll be something else on top of it of course

PRESIDENT. At that precise moment Sophie Auzanneau did you love him?

SOPHIE. I don't know

PRESIDENT. I doubt it will do you any good to retreat into silence

SOPHIE. I say what I know

PRESIDENT. The Court is trying to understand

MME. AUZANNEAU. That way when we're old *you* won't forget *us* in our old age

PRESIDENT. You're anxious for us to believe you

So give us an exact account of how your relationship
with Xavier Bergeret began

SOPHIE. He followed me

He suggested we went for a drink

He invited me back to his place to have some fresh
grilled sardines

I told him I wasn't too keen on his sardines

PRESIDENT. At your very first meeting a certain pattern
was established in the contact between you

You switch him on then you switch him off in a game
of cat and mouse

SOPHIE. I was talking about sardines

He was quite put out he didn't know what to do with
his hands so I pressed them over my breasts and then
we went to his place to go to bed

PRESIDENT. Was it he who proposed this?

SOPHIE. I don't remember

PRESIDENT. Whichever way it was you weren't embar-
rassed? Spending the night with a young man you'd
never seen before that day?

SOPHIE. It was pleasure

PRESIDENT. Pleasure comes easily to you

I insist on order in this Court

You take your pleasure with Bergeret pleasure with
Colonna then with Legouit and I pass over the others

I suppose when you were sixteen Colonel Schlessinger
the Doctor in the German army gave you pleasure just
as easily

MME. AUZANNEAU. Your papa has sacrificed a lot for
you and you've never given him a single word of
thanks

He doesn't ask for much

When he patched that pear tree together who do you
think he did it for?
Who does the work that pays for your room in Lille
your registration fees your dissecting instruments and
all those books and dictionaries?
When we sent your elder brother to university he wrote
us this letter I've always kept and I must have read it to
you a hundred times

(The bed in XAVIER's room in Lille.)

SOPHIE. It was the tree I used to climb when I was small
   I'd stay there for hours curled up in the fork where the
   three big branches met
   My cat used to come too when she felt like it and snug-
   gle down in my lap I'd tickle her behind the ears and
   when *I* felt like it I'd pick a pear that still wasn't ripe
   and dig my teeth in
   There in my nest I was invincible
XAVIER. Invisible you mean
SOPHIE. Invincible because I was out of sight
XAVIER. You've always liked to remain unseen
   Yet you'll get up to anything to draw attention to your-
   self?
SOPHIE. It's bliss
   To hide myself away
   No Xavier
   I don't love you as much as you love me
PRESIDENT. He insisted you should marry him
XAVIER. You play hide and seek with yourself
   You hide from your own feelings
   I can see what you refuse to see
SOPHIE. What do you see?

XAVIER. That you love me

   I'll make you see it

   We'll get married and you'll see

SOPHIE. I don't know

XAVIER. The ice will melt

SOPHIE. You'll be my tree

XAVIER. Will you then?

SOPHIE. And the storm will come

XAVIER. You're devastating

DR. HAUDEBOURG. She betrays a particular form of instability which is the signal characteristic of an unbalanced mind she's impulsive irascible and if you add to that strong signs of degeneration on the maternal side of her family

SOPHIE. I don't want to make you unhappy

DR. HAUDEBOURG. The concomitance of these two observations has led us to the conclusion that this is a case of diminished responsibility

XAVIER. I want to make you happy

PUBLIC PROSECUTOR. She has told us Doctor that she fired in cold blood you speak of her "irascibility" how did you get that idea?

DR. HAUDEBOURG. Let's call it "an irascible state of mind" it makes no difference she is irascible by nature but may still maintain a certain coolness in any given act

   Psychiatry anyway is not a mathematical science

SOPHIE. You're so terribly tender and gentle with me

XAVIER. And you don't like it?

SOPHIE. I'm not used to it

   Are you taking me to a film?

   I want to smooch at the flicks

XAVIER. You're still not giving me an answer

SOPHIE. Afterwards we'll see

LUBET. So we can see Members of the Jury that even
before the fatal act of physical liquidation
There was a deliberate attempt at psychological degra-
dation the breaking down of a human being whose one
weakness was an attachment to certain values
A precious metal that will be attacked insidiously by an
acid which will prove fatal to it

MME. GUIBOT. She was a chilly mortal too
Not a mollycoddle I mean there's a difference she used
to roll herself up without a stitch on in three thick blan-
kets even in the summer
Her cat in bed with her
And giggle

(COLONNA's bedroom in Lille.)

XAVIER. I'm intruding on your privacy Monsieur Col-
lonna

COLONNA. What can I do for you Bergeret?
At this hour I must say

MME. GUIBOT. Sometimes there were two or three people in her room peals of laughter and hers was the loudest

XAVIER. Is Sophie here?

COLONNA. I'm sorry Sophie who?

XAVIER. Sophie Auzanneau

COLONNA. Auzanneau? What an idea

XAVIER. It's about her I've come to see you
She's been seen with you quite a lot she doesn't hide it
I'm interested in her it's not a secret we've been to-
gether for over a year I want to know what's going on
I have a right to know

COLONNA. Ask her

XAVIER. She says she's a free agent

COLONNA. If that's what she thinks

XAVIER. But you see it's not what she thinks she tells me

COLONNA. What can I do about it?

XAVIER. You can tell me if you love her if you're think-ing of marriage *(COLONNA smiles and holds out his hand. Handshake. XAVIER leaves.)*

(SOPHIE emerges from the cupboard, naked, wrapped in a blanket. Roaring with laughter. She stops laughing abruptly and shivers.)

SOPHIE. I'm cold warm me up

COLONNA. But it's quite hot in here

SOPHIE. I'm always cold

   (COLONNA wraps her in two more blankets, lifts her up and lays her on the bed. Then he lies down beside her.)

   Shall we make some tea? Piping hot

   I think I love him

COLONNA. Yes

SOPHIE. You think so too?

   At least *you* don't love me that's a relief

   And you're not wanting to marry me

COLONNA. I haven't exactly said I don't love you

SOPHIE. It would be a relief if you did

COLONNA. China Tea? Ceylon?

   Darjeeling?

   You crying?

SOPHIE. I feel so miserable

COLONNA. You didn't answer

   Darjeeling?

SOPHIE. Is that what you asked me?

COLONNA. Just now

SOPHIE. I don't know anything any more

Oh I don't know what I want

COLONNA. And I made some Darjeeling

My relationship with Mademoiselle Auzanneau went on for three weeks perhaps a month it was some time before the tragedy I wonder what I'm doing here I really didn't know her well enough to be able to pass judgement on her

The news was such a shock I may have made certain remarks but I realise now time has passed that they have little bearing on the truth

For me she was a good companion rather too intense at times it's been said it was self-interest that made her turn to me

Nothing could be further from the truth

To be in my good books as her examiner no truth in that at all I have never been a member of any board of examiners

CANCÉ. What were you feeling?

COLONNA. Feeling for her?

PRESIDENT. I must have order in the Court

CANCÉ. About her

COLONNA. About her? An unlucky sort of girl

PRESIDENT. I must ask the witness to be good enough to wait until public order is restored before proceeding with his evidence

COLONNA. She chased after a love she was never able to find it's undeniable she was thrown off course by some of the men who also chased after her and indulged in blackmail to win her consent that also helped to influence her behaviour

CANCÉ. Thank you

PRESIDENT. Are there other witnesses for the defence to call?

You were born?

SOPHIE. On March the 11th 1927 at Dunkirk

PRESIDENT. Your father ran a plumbing and roofing business and your mother just kept house

(In front of the Faculty of Medicine in Lille.)

CLAUDETTE. Coming?

PRESIDENT. Though she helped to keep her husband's accounts

SOPHIE. Where?

CLAUDETTE. For a walk

SOPHIE. I'm in the dumps

PRESIDENT. You appear to have been your parents' favourite child yet you'll tell us you lacked affection

Your father thought you were too brainy your mother didn't understand you is that correct?

CLAUDETTE. But you don't mind do you?

SOPHIE. He got through and I got a resit I won't put up with this separation I'm going to see him

CLAUDETTE. He's determined to go to Paris?

SOPHIE. I'll tell him I'm going with him

CLAUDETTE. Sure you know what you want to do?

CANCÉ. Sometimes up in your pear tree you took a book with you?

SOPHIE. I always kept a book in the pocket of my dungarees

CANCÉ. Do you remember any of the titles?

SOPHIE. *Gone With The Wind*

PRESIDENT. Came our defeat and the ensuing Occupation it seems your father was not unduly affected by these events

CANCÉ. Romances? Novels?

SOPHIE. *Pride and Prejudice For Whom the Bell Tolls*

PRESIDENT. In 1940 you were thirteen years old two of your three brothers were killed one on the submarine he commanded the other during an air force exercise in 1941 when you were fourteen you were seen on the terrace of a café wearing a bathing costume in the company of German sailors

SOPHIE. *The Sun Also Rises* usually American novels

PRESIDENT. And before you reached fifteen you went horse-riding with the Commander of the Occupation Forces one evening you go out for a walk arm in arm with a soldier of the Wehrmacht and you're stopped by a policeman who makes out a report the Headmistress of your school is stirred into action

Discreet measures were apparently taken which led to the defendant's expulsion after which she seems to have pursued her studies at home

CANCÉ. I have proof that this assertion is incorrect Monsieur le Président and I herewith submit the deposition of the Headmaster of the school not you notice the so-called Headmistress according to which Sophie Auzanneau was never excluded from his *lycée* during the Occupation

This is by no means the only example in this case of what would appear to be manipulation of the facts

PRESIDENT. I will not allow these proceedings to break the tradition of calm deliberation alone conducive to the pursuit of justice and the uncovering of the truth

(On a pavement in Lille.)

SOPHIE. Did you treat yourself to a new suit? It must be
    a must
    When one's going to make one's first appearance in
    Paris
    Turn around take a few steps it changes the way you
    walk
    A bit loose round the shoulders
XAVIER. It was agony choosing it
SOPHIE. You should have taken me with you
    Oh no that back's no good at all
XAVIER. What?
SOPHIE. The jacket doesn't hang straight
XAVIER. Sophie
SOPHIE. What?
XAVIER. You're doing this on purpose we were meant
    not to meet again
SOPHIE. Maybe I am maybe I've been too hard on you
    I didn't know how I stood with you it took me time to
    find out
    Now I know
XAVIER. Now it's too late
PRESIDENT. All your friends have said you were more
    annoyed than upset by this break-up
SOPHIE. Words I don't know what they mean
CANCÉ. Sophie Auzanneau fell in love with Xavier Ber-
    geret at roughly the same moment as he stopped loving her
SOPHIE. I was in despair
LUBET. A black comedy of despair
CANCÉ. Since a man died I'd call it a tragedy
LUBET. A comedy at the first I repeat

A sinister comedy fabricated from start to finish out of pique

A carefully rehearsed performance inspired by blighted hope and by egocentric malice of the most savage and contemptible kind

SOPHIE. I'd like to try and say I'd like you to believe me

LUBET. In despair let's see what you did in your desperation

You went by train to Austria and as soon as you set foot in Vienna in great despair you find the real thing a love affair this time with a Monsieur Legouit a French engineer on assignment

SOPHIE. I'd like to try and explain I'd always lived at home with my mother and father afraid to show my feelings

I never found it easy to talk about my personal problems to people who took no interest

PRESIDENT. But surely your mother would have noticed something

SOPHIE. Those who are closest to you sir may be the last ones to know you really well

In my home somehow we always lived cut off from one another you'd never imagine how cold my father was

LUBET. How I ask is this relevant to your idyllic Austrian romance?

SOPHIE. When I was small I thought he didn't love me at all so whether I felt happy or not I'd got into the habit of keeping it all to myself

(SOPHIE's room in Lille.)

CLAUDETTE. Why yes I promise you

SOPHIE. And he talked about me?

    He hasn't forgotten me?

CLAUDETTE. Goodness I can hardly believe how you look

    What a transformation

SOPHIE. Hang on I'll ask Madame Guibot to make us a cup of tea

    What did he say Claudette tell me everything he said

PRESIDENT. In 1944 you were seventeen it was the end of the war the Allies had surrounded Dunkirk

CLAUDETTE. He was worried about you how things were going for you

    And what you'd drifted into

    He was hoping you hadn't been left on your own that there was someone to take care of you

PRESIDENT. The German authorities had all the civilians evacuated but you stayed on with your father

SOPHIE. No I had a room in the military hospital

CLAUDETTE. He was afraid you'd go to pieces

PRESIDENT. The hospital for the Wehrmacht

SOPHIE. He didn't say he'd like to well I don't know

CLAUDETTE. See you again? Oh no he said

    It was over well and truly over he told me he'd got engaged to a girl called Francine

    It seems to be a practical arrangement you know not a shattering affair

    He'd had his share of grand passion he said

    Settling down I guess

SOPHIE. Tell me his address

PRESIDENT. There you come across a Colonel in the Medical Corps Doctor Schlessinger a man of fifty-five you were seventeen and you became his mistress

CLAUDETTE. I don't know his address

SOPHIE. You're lying

CLAUDETTE. Perhaps you'll meet again in a few years' time

You'll both have settled down and you'll be swapping notes about the kids you've each had

But now if you take my advice pack it in

SOPHIE. You do know his address

CLAUDETTE. He usually confides in me he's fond of me but I could tell he was on his guard he knows I'm your closest friend

SOPHIE. His address

PRESIDENT. The Allies' final onslaught brought the conflict to an end

CLAUDETTE. Normally he would have told me his address

We mustn't let our paths cross again

SOPHIE. He said that

PRESIDENT. But you are never to lose sight of your Doctor the Colonel you write to him and you go and see him at Ulm in August 1950

LUBET. Only a few months before the crime

SOPHIE. I've simply got to see him Claudette

LUBET. A crime that's presented to us as a crime of passion

CLAUDETTE. It's a bit late to wake up to him now

LUBET. What did she want from him?

Money no doubt.

SOPHIE. I didn't realise

LUBET. It's all one to Sophie Auzanneau which lover she pursues

SOPHIE. Can you lend me two thousand francs?

LUBET. Young or old German or French

SOPHIE. For the train fare

I'll pay you back in a week I'm going to my parents for my birthday there's an envelope waiting for me with some cash

LUBET. She never returned the loan of course

CLAUDETTE. I'm sure she would if events had turned out differently

SOPHIE. Let me have the two thousand francs

CLAUDETTE. Now you've got this other bloke after what you tell me he's a decent sort he's got a good position and he wants what's best for you

Go and live abroad for a while

Vienna's a lovely city

What's his name?

SOPHIE. Legouit

Just now I can't think about Legouit

CLAUDETTE. He's in love with you and you say you love him

Turn the page

SOPHIE. I get my pages mixed up

I need that address

CLAUDETTE. You never stopped telling him you weren't the wife for him

You made him believe it in the end

SOPHIE. Oh my knees I'll go on my knees to him

Oh Claudette today I'm ready to agree to anything

I'll be the wife he's dreamed of

PRESIDENT. You arrived at the Gare du Nord

Then what did you do?

SOPHIE. I went straight to his place

PRESIDENT. You hadn't seen him for

SOPHIE. Eighteen months

LUBET. I note Monsieur le President that the defendant contradicts herself in a previous statement she made it

clear it was not until the morning of the following day
that she charged in on Bergeret having spent the night
at a hotel

SOPHIE. I hadn't the money for a hotel room

I went straight to his place

PRESIDENT. And then what?

SOPHIE. He let me in

PRESIDENT. What happened next?

SOPHIE. We had supper

PRESIDENT. In his room?

SOPHIE. Yes

PUBLIC PROSECUTOR. The events leading up to this
bloodbath have now been pieced together

It was all worked out in advance down to the smallest
detail the admissions made at this hearing?

All calculated

A bloodbath and a torrent of lies

There may be talk of other affairs but I tell you no
affair is quite like any other and Members of the Jury
you weren't party to them anyway so let us stick to our
affair and ignore all the rest

*(The hospital in Dunkirk. SOPHIE is wearing a white
coat.)*

DR. SCHLESSINGER. What is there to eat?

SOPHIE. You look tired

DR. SCHLESSINGER. You're my one consolation

Today they arrived in droves badly wounded

SOPHIE. Young Wolfgang died spitting blood

I held his hand

DR. SCHLESSINGER. There should be more little French
girls warm-hearted like you

Now you can come and hop on my lap
So I can give my little kitten a cuddle
SOPHIE. Gently now
You're going to lose this war
DR. SCHLESSINGER. Never
SOPHIE. And I shall lose you
Will you take me with you?
DR. SCHLESSINGER. What would Frau Schlessinger say?
PUBLIC PROSECUTOR. I oppose and reject any plea for
diminished responsibility or extenuating circumstances
our distinguished experts have made much of her tem-
peramental character but I tell you these experts have
misread the motive
Sophie was hell-bent on destroying any chance of hap-
piness because Sophie is a monster
Wasn't she a monster already as an adolescent when
she linked up with our invaders?
Between them and her there was a great affinity
And isn't she still a monster when the day before her
trial is due to start in the very last moments before her
feigned attempt at suicide she makes out a will in fa-
vour of who you may ask? In the name of a woman
sentenced to hard labour for life
A woman who had killed her first child aged eighteen
months and five years later a second one and in both
cases claimed that their death was accidental
Once again Sophie Auzanneau found a great affinity
with this odious woman
Not without reason did Xavier Bergeret say she was
devastating
So this death that she brought upon him

(XAVIER'S room in Paris.)

XAVIER. God

   What are you doing here?

PUBLIC PROSECUTOR. I now call down upon her

SOPHIE. Can I sit down?

XAVIER. Sit

PUBLIC PROSECUTOR. Not in the smallest measure

SOPHIE. It's nice for you here

XAVIER. Think so?

SOPHIE. It's cheerful like you

PUBLIC PROSECUTOR. Can I find it in my heart to forgive her

   In defence of humanity and our feeble hopes of happiness I demand for this monster the ultimate penalty

CANCÉ. I stand up alone

   To face these extravagant allegations

   For this is all wild exaggeration and the very enormity
   of it weighs me down like a cloak of lead

SOPHIE. Have you got a bathroom too?

XAVIER. See for yourself

SOPHIE. All you need eh you haven't changed

XAVIER. Nor you

SOPHIE. I have

XAVIER. Still got your cat?

SOPHIE. Madame Guibot looks after her

   You don't hear too much noise from the traffic is this
   new?

XAVIER. This kit

   A friend in electronics put it together for me

SOPHIE. Do you listen to lots of music?

   Do you still believe there are only three or four possi-
   ble situations?

XAVIER. With variations

SOPHIE. Did you learn in the end

How to do your own ironing?

Can I take my shoes off?

XAVIER. Where have you come from?

SOPHIE. Gare du Nord

XAVIER. Who gave you the address?

SOPHIE. Are you cross?

XAVIER. No

It's just that we agreed

SOPHIE. I know

You want me to go?

XAVIER. You've taken your shoes off

So stay for a while

SOPHIE. Can I invite you to supper?

XAVIER. I'm inviting you there's left-overs in the fridge

LUBET. Lies lies lies a barrage of lies

PRESIDENT. If you don't mind Maître I have not yet fin-
ished the cross-examination

LUBET. On the morning of the 7th of March she took
Xavier by surprise at No. 25 rue de l'Abbé Groult

The address she'd wrung out of her friend as we heard

Some minutes later she left having realised the break
was beyond repair

As she went out she made the following remark "if
that's the way it is all I can do now is disappear"

We know because next day Xavier repeated it word for
word to his fiancée Francine

These Monsieur le Président are the facts

PRESIDENT. For heaven's sake Maître let us take things
one at a time

You took a room in a hotel

SOPHIE. I took the metro at the Gare du Nord and went
straight to his place

We had supper in his room

PRESIDENT. What did you talk about?

SOPHIE. Nothing of importance

PRESIDENT. You hadn't seen him for eighteen months you say you were madly in love with him and you spoke of nothing of importance?

SOPHIE. Yes but we spent the night together

PRESIDENT. I will have order in this Court

LUBET. So when you were asked by the police why didn't you mention this before?

SOPHIE. I didn't want to tell anyone about it

I just said he'd kissed me the way he used to

PUBLIC PROSECUTOR. I rather think you kept quiet about it because you weren't sure that Bergeret was dead and you felt he might have denied it

Only when you found you really had killed him did it occur to you to fabricate a story to make it look more like a crime of passion

So this night you spent together is pure invention

CANCÉ. Who is inventing making up stories now?

Public Prosecutor sir you reduce me to despair your legal procedure is so finely tuned in such good working order that it would leave me defenceless were it not for my open mind my probity

So I am uneasy

In the course of my professional career I have tried to come to terms with the clients I defend get to like them for what they are try and understand them

And you Members of the Jury should make an effort to understand too

By looking closely into yourselves at your own faults your own misgivings

And if it so happens you can find none then by considering the failings and misfortunes of others

PRESIDENT. And you returned to Lille?

SOPHIE. Yes the day after

PRESIDENT. This time it is Madame Guibot your
    landlady's evidence which enlightens us

    Madame Guibot was more than a landlady to you

    Someone you could confide in not unlike an accom-
    plice?

MME. GUIBOT. Me an accomplice sir?

PRESIDENT. Don't misunderstand me I know you sent
    that telegram and warned the boy's father by telephone
    you did the right and proper thing

    But you felt some sympathy for your tenant a sort of
    indulgence almost motherly

    You understood her as it seems her own mother had
    never done

(DR. SCHLESSINGER's surgery at Ulm.)

DR. SCHLESSINGER. What an absolutely wonderful sur-
    prise

    My little ray of sunshine

SOPHIE. My cavalier my first one

DR. SCHLESSINGER. Problems?

SOPHIE. Bernd

    I simply had to see you

DR. SCHLESSINGER. Some special reason?

SOPHIE. I miss you terribly

    Every single day

DR. SCHLESSINGER. I'm an old quack an old Boche
    unappetising at that

    And you're a splendid young woman of twenty-three

    My kitten's grown into a tigress

SOPHIE. Don't joke about it

If the world was a better place
We'd be living together

DR. SCHLESSINGER. Recognise this pebble?

SOPHIE. The Doctor still keeps it in his pocket?

DR. SCHLESSINGER. Now you're a doctor too?

SOPHIE. No

DR. SCHLESSINGER. Married?

SOPHIE. No

DR. SCHLESSINGER. What about that boy who wanted to marry you and you wouldn't?

SOPHIE. Now he doesn't want to and I do

DR. SCHLESSINGER. So the world is a pretty awful place
Let's change it

SOPHIE. We'll rub it out and start again

DR. SCHLESSINGER. Where have you just come from? Lille? Paris?

SOPHIE. I'm living in Vienna with a very nice man who says he never fell for anyone like me before
Bernd I want to stay here with you for a day or two

DR. SCHLESSINGER. That won't be too easy with Frau Schlessinger around

SOPHIE. I don't mind a hotel if I can see you for an hour every day
You've nothing to fear from me Bernd
I'm not wicked or mad
It's just that I must

DR. SCHLESSINGER. And your Viennese gentleman?

SOPHIE. Do you know Vienna Bernd?
A gingerbread city a long way from the sea
A part of it's subsiding and my gentleman's got the job of underpinning it

He wants us to get married I told him I needed a few
days away to think it over

DR. SCHLESSINGER. You haven't learnt much

SOPHIE. I don't know anything Bernd any more

DR. SCHLESSINGER. My tigress can't decide which
way to jump next

SOPHIE. Any nice forests round here?

DR. SCHLESSINGER. I've heard tales of woods in Vienna

SOPHIE. Not even a tree just one tree?

PRESIDENT. Right in front of him
Why did you throw yourself under his very eyes into
the arms of Monsieur Colonna a man you didn't love?
To taunt him? Or just out of cruelty?

SOPHIE. Can you know in advance if love will come?

PRESIDENT. Xavier knew he was in love with you but
you didn't love him you told us yourself what you felt
for him was not love but affection so why keep him on
the hook for so long?

SOPHIE. It's true my feelings weren't the same as his I
thought at the time we couldn't ever be happy together
At least I didn't realise we could
But then I came to see I was really in love

PRESIDENT. All the more surprising then if you were so
fond of him
All the more surprising that you should get involved
with this engineer this Monsieur Legouit in Austria
who you then walked out on to go and spend a few
days at Ulm with your former lover Doctor Schlessinger
One can't help wondering who you're in love with
A little order Ladies and Gentlemen in this courtroom

SOPHIE. If there was no hope for me with Bergeret I had
to get fixed up with someone else I'd got it wrong once
already

It had made me very unhappy I didn't want to make
another mistake I wasn't sure I was in love with
Legouit

PRESIDENT. That is not the impression one gets when
reading your letters to him let me quote from one

"This is the first time making some man happy or seeing that he's happy for some other reason

Has meant more to me

Than my own self-gratification"

SOPHIE. I never realised

Anyway it didn't stop me thinking about Bergeret

PUBLIC PROSECUTOR. Didn't you say that with pa-
tience your fidelity would bring Bergeret round?

One can't help wondering what you understand by fidelity

SOPHIE. It's hard to explain

PRESIDENT. Laughter in this court is out of place

MME. GUIBOT. And then I put my hand in her bag and
pulled out the bottle that contained the fatal concoction

Your young gentleman's all of a piece I told her he's
straight as they come

He was in love with you you put him off so he broke it
off

PRESIDENT. A good summing-up

MME. GUIBOT. And I pointed out there were other fish
to fry

She knew there were others all right

That all happened a fortnight after they broke up and he
moved to Paris he came back to Lille for a day or two
she found out and wanted to talk to him he agreed to

meet her but he refused to take up with her again and
she threatened to poison herself Monsieur Xavier got
into a state and came in to warn me I rushed upstairs
fast as I could with my rheumatics

(SOPHIE's room in Lille.)

MME. GUIBOT. Where's your handbag?

SOPHIE. Here

MME. GUIBOT. What is it?

SOPHIE. Cyanide

MME. GUIBOT. Better have a good cry than swallow this
muck

SOPHIE. They say it's got a nasty taste

I've no choice it's all too much for me there's no way
out leave me alone

MME. GUIBOT. I don't remember what I said next but
her tears started so I stroked her hair and she fell asleep
with her head on my shoulder

LUBET. Obviously a put-up job a sly bit of blackmail

CANCÉ. That no one should remain in ignorance

When Monsieur Auzanneau heard what his daughter
had done he took his own life he was found with a gas
pipe in his mouth his body full of ether

Earlier on he had sent Monsieur Bergeret a letter of
excuse and condolence

SOPHIE. In my family no one ever seems to die a natural
death

PRESIDENT. You can judge for yourselves how genuine
were her attempts at suicide

May I recall the report drawn up by Doctor Paul following the attempt which forced us into an adjournment

Sophie Auzanneau made good use of her medical knowledge first she applied a tourniquet to her left fore-arm then with a needle or a piece of broken glass we're not quite sure which she cut clean into the radial vein

She lost about a litre of blood and was found comatose in her cell at six o'clock this morning when I saw her at ten she was still in the same condition

Pulse rate impossible to count blood pressure under six

But next morning she had recovered enough of her strength and her mental faculties to compose a letter she addressed to me which reads as follows

"I am obliged to write this letter in the dark as I don't want to switch the night light on

I hope Monsieur and Madame Bergeret will forgive me if they can and take pity on my mother I'm sorry for all I've done

I bitterly regret that I killed him

But I will not submit to a system of justice devoid of all dignity I refuse to be tried in public in front of a crowd that reminds me of the howling mobs of the Revolution my trial ought to have been held *in camera* I'm glad I've been able to thwart the officials who set the stage for this masquerade"

I shall not ask you Sophie Auzanneau whether you have had second thoughts about this scurrilous attack on the law

PUBLIC PROSECUTOR. To slow the law down that above all was your strategy Sophie Auzanneau to drag it all out

Thanks to your squalid performance you have gained seven weeks

CANCÉ. I object to this interpretation from the representa-
tive of the State I too have received a letter from my
client

A heart-rending one

Which with your permission I shall not make public

PRESIDENT. In the moments that followed the crime because we have to return to that

Did you Sophie Auzanneau really intend to put an end
to your life?

Or was it rather

To use your own words

An attempt to set the stage?

Would our expert like to throw some light on this
point?

DR. HAUDEBOURG. For Sophie Auzanneau there seems
to be something normal and logical about suicide she
was brought up to think like this

In our psychiatric report we specifically referred to it as
a theatrical suicide and yes we chose the expression
with care

We called it theatrical to draw attention to its flamboy-
ance and not to say it was simulated

(The bed in XAVIER's room in Lille.)

SOPHIE. Xavier

XAVIER. Yes

SOPHIE. I feel sleepy

XAVIER. Relax with my arms round you

SOPHIE. In your arms yes

And not wake up again

Why is everything so difficult?

Why does it hurt so?

Why do I hurt you so much?

How long is this going to last?

LUBET. I'm not going to muddy the issue

When a spade is a spade

I'm outspoken enough to say so

The defence is engaged in a subtle manoeuvre designed
to trap you into understanding while at the same time
befogging you in clouds of mystification

XAVIER. You're all snuggled up but you're tensed up too

How can you

If only you could let yourself go

SOPHIE. Let myself go

Yes

If you knew how I'd like to

But then you know I can't

I can't

LUBET. The defence prefers to dwell in that somewhat
disturbing twilight zone where the line dividing what is
from what is not becomes blurred

SOPHIE. Can you hear

The storm

About to cause havoc in the garden?

Papa had to get up in the middle of the night

I'm afraid

XAVIER. Afraid of what? I'm here

SOPHIE. Of myself

Of everything

I should never have told you about the sardines

The trunk splits and the branch gets broken

My cat has slipped under the netting

Gone a-roving

And do I love you?

Do you love me?

    Words that don't come neat in their little compartments
    But go rolling rolling on

LUBET. Understanding what escapes all understanding of
    course so you are no longer able to pass judgement

    Because judgement ah Members of the Jury judgement

SOPHIE. Like a pebble

    You ought to break me open to find out what's inside

LUBET. Judgement as André Malraux said is clearly the
    negation of understanding

    Never mind if I break the spell and drag you back to
    earth

    There one can understand and pass judgement in the
    full light of day

SOPHIE. Break me with your teeth

    Bite me

    Hard

    Where am I? Who is it?

XAVIER. It's me

    And it's you

    Here

SOPHIE. Where?

    One day you know I'll kill you

    To simplify

XAVIER. What will that simplify?

SOPHIE. Do you know why you love me?

XAVIER. I know how it all began

    I loved your laugh before I loved your face

    In the large lecture-room I could sometimes hear this
    laugh coming from a bench behind me

SOPHIE. When did you find out which face it belonged
    to?

XAVIER. One day I followed a girl out of the lecture-
    room she was beautiful and on the boulevard between

two rows of plane trees she said to me chance and fate
are two sides of the same coin

It stuck in my mind you see because then she laughed
and I recognised the laugh I'd heard behind me

A laugh that has nothing to do with a sense of humour

SOPHIE. She doesn't have a sense of humour?

XAVIER. None at all

SOPHIE. So she can't enjoy a joke

What if the whole of her life was a joke?

XAVIER. She blew hot and cold

Is that what I loved about her?

SOPHIE. Look

It's going to be fine today

It'll be the most beautiful day

To learn how to love loving perhaps

I hope one can learn how I do so want

To be able to love

LUBET. You don't need to make up your minds about
whether a crime was committed or who the guilty party
is the admissions already made by the defendant have
relieved us of this obligation

You only have to resolve two problems premeditation
and mitigating circumstances and your response will
depend upon the personal conviction you have each of
you formed concerning the motives for the crime

What the defence puts forward is woolly and obscure

Attempting to lead you astray

Whereas I shall demonstrate

XAVIER. That's what I like you're the one I want

SOPHIE. But I hurt you

XAVIER. The first night you spent with me

You said I was hurting you

LUBET. I shall prove that the one and only motive for the
crime was self-interest

(At the Auzanneaus' house in Lille.)

M. AUZANNEAU. You're not going to like this much
Though with you one can never tell
Henri is dead.
SOPHIE. I'm often like that
Henri who?
M. AUZANNEAU. Your brother
MME. AUZANNEAU. She was always at loggerheads
with her elder brother
M. AUZANNEAU. His submarine has been sunk
MME. AUZANNEAU. With the other one it wasn't the
same
She seems to have grieved for him
M. AUZANNEAU. She showed nothing

(SOPHIE's room in Lille.)

CLAUDETTE. Why?
SOPHIE. Yes why do you think he wanted to know who
was sleeping with me?
CLAUDETTE. His affair with you may be at an end but
that doesn't stop him you know still taking an interest
in you
MME. AUZANNEAU. Our little girl was precocious emo-
tionally
M. AUZANNEAU. The war didn't help
SOPHIE. Did you feel he was jealous?
CLAUDETTE. Of course a touch of jealousy it's a natural
reaction

Anyone would think it's good news I'm bringing you
But Sophie no he won't see you any more he's getting
married it's over
LUBET. Self-interest
The crime of an opportunist a money-grubbing woman
set on marriage
Whose interest in men is stimulated only by their status
A fortune-hunter
If she got Xavier in her clutches it's because Xavier
was the most desirable and if she left him later it's be-
cause he wouldn't have her any more
The men she tried to seduce after that also appealed to
her only because of their money or their position Col-
onna Legouit
She discovers that the first man is not the marrying
type and the business prospects of the second didn't
equal her expectations
Then she wants to go back to Xavier Bergeret
But the young man is unshakeable he has made up his
mind he gets engaged to Francine no hope left there
So she reached her decision
Every avenue is closed to her and she will not allow
this man to seize his chance of happiness
She will shoot him down
With a revolver in her pocket she waits for him in the
entrance to his block of flats
Like a killer
Is this your drama of love?
She has thought it all out
She fires the first bullet into his back he collapses she
walks all round the body
Fires a second time at his forehead

Then the *coup de grâce* at zero range into his temple
Of course it's only a hypothesis

PUBLIC PROSECUTOR. On a café terrace in her bathing
costume in the company of German sailors

(A café terrace in Paris.)

CORNAILLE. Don't let her in

XAVIER. You mustn't all drop her completely or she'll
just let herself drift

MME. GUIBOT. I wouldn't say I'd had a premonition but
I'd use a cup of tea as an excuse
At odd times I'd go upstairs and suggest a cup of tea
On her bed I saw a will a paper anyway and on it she'd
written will

CORNAILLE. He was an honest frank straightforward fellow incapable of deception

LACHAUD. A gentleman that's the word from a united
family his father was a vet at Saint-Omer

MME. GUIBOT. She must have tiptoed down the stairs I
never heard her come down
She'd been lying up there all depressed for a couple of
days and then suddenly no one there not even her shop-
ping-bag

CLAUDETTE. It was as if something had made her happy
Yes at that moment there was a change in her character

MME. GUIBOT. I sent my telegram off

CLAUDETTE. She didn't seem so strange to me not so
hard
I was much more drawn to her.

MME. GUIBOT. The telephone call to his father too
To Saint-Omer where he had his clinic

CORNAILLE. He loved her " 'tis pity she's a whore" he said to me one day but that remark should be taken sir as typical of a student for us

It didn't have the same literal meaning a policeman would give it

LACHAUD. Though he really had grown away from her there was a lingering trace of compassion

PRESIDENT. Your past life is what one might call erratic tempestuous even

MME. GUIBOT. I used to do her washing for her

One morning when I took her clean clothes back there she was starkers in bed she always used to sleep in her birthday suit even in the winter with ten below freezing outside

Someone came in without knocking it was Monsieur Xavier he slipped into bed beside her fully dressed the two of them never took no notice of me

She asked me if I'd bring up two cups of tea

PUBLIC PROSECUTOR. So now we can trace in ghastly clarity the emergence of this blackguardly scheme in which every step was calculated

She didn't take the lift

She climbed the stairs from one floor to the next with a brief pause perhaps on each landing

In order to rehearse every move she was about to make With him unbeknowing upstairs

And her

With her foot in the door in case he should reject her once more

It's terrifying

At least let us not be afraid to call things by their proper name this is the unscrupulous perfidy of a

woman who had worked everything out weighed up all
the pros and cons

CORNAILLE. He had warned me never to give her his
address

LACHAUD. We were on our guard

CORNAILLE. We knew she was proud intelligent romantic

LACHAUD. But we never thought her capable of this

(DR. SCHLESSINGER's surgery at Ulm.)

SOPHIE. I feel tired Bernd

DR. SCHLESSINGER. I told Frau Schlessinger I had to
perform an operation this evening
Till late at night

SOPHIE. Say something nice to me

CORNAILLE. Xavier was a great guy and Sophie Auzanneau wasn't the kind of girl a fellow like him could
take as a wife

DR. SCHLESSINGER. In the hospital at Dunkirk there
was a little parrot do you remember?

SOPHIE. My cat used to prowl around him ferociously
While the bombs were dropping

LACHAUD. Sophie Auzanneau wasn't good enough for
Xavier
Xavier reproached her with what we all blamed her for
betraying him making a fool of him over Colonna and
the rest
All she ever wanted was to do her own thing

SOPHIE. Maybe in my whole life I've never been happier

(SOPHIE's room in Lille.)

XAVIER. Just over a year ago I asked you to be my wife

In spite of all that's happened I'm asking you again
today

FRANCINE. He told me at once that he'd known this
woman but it was over

Since he first got to know me I'm sure absolutely positive he hasn't seen her again

LACHAUD. It's true I never had much sympathy for her
myself

PRESIDENT. So I'd like to ask you whether in your con-
cern for justice this feeling of repulsion for her has
been moderated?

SOPHIE. No Xavier don't ask me that

XAVIER. Is this your last word?

LACHAUD. Did I mention repulsion?

In any case I'm sure even Xavier

Wouldn't approve of all this (*With a slight gesture
around him.*)

PUBLIC PROSECUTOR. Wouldn't approve of all this? Aha.

But he must have foreseen it all and that must be right
if I'm to believe your own evidence for that telegram
was passed on to you with the words

May I ask you to repeat them?

LACHAUD. "If anything happens to me"

PUBLIC PROSECUTOR. And in fact didn't something
happen to him?

Something premeditated

LUBET. The life of this young man

PUBLIC PROSECUTOR. Can there be any doubt about
it?

LUBET. Like all those who are really strong he was honest and upright

The happiness of that united family yes who had everything going for them

Has all been swept away destroyed annihilated by Sophie Auzanneau's criminal act

Death broken lives indescribable suffering and it's all
due to you Sophie Auzanneau though you seem hardly
aware of it

Obsessed as you are with yourself

Hour after hour month after month we've been hanging
on your lips for one word of regret or excuse hoping
for a hint of repentance in your eyes

But your mouth has been silent your eyes have shown
nothing but the glint of a hard heart

So don't expect either pardon or mercy from us

SOPHIE. You'd laugh at my landlady

Bernd she watches over me with a gruff kindness I
never knew at home

She does my washing for me and brings me tea

DR. SCHLESSINGER. You let it get cold you always
have you always say you like it piping hot

Then you leave it for hours to get cold

(At the Auzanneaus' house at Dunkirk.)

MME. AUZANNEAU. She's twenty-four an age when
one should think about marriage it's time she settled
down

A postcard from her she's all right and she'll be here as
usual for her birthday

SOPHIE. She loves telling me off when are you going to
stop chasing around like an Amazon?

She's convinced the Amazons are natives a tribe of
wild women who are cannibals in South America

M. AUZANNEAU. We spent enough on her education
didn't we?

SOPHIE. Yet at the same time I get the feeling she'd protect me if anyone tried to hurt me

MME. AUZANNEAU. We did all we could the same as we would for the others

CANCÉ. But there you have it she'd been told never to show her feelings in her face she was taught to distrust people's faces

DR. SCHLESSINGER. I never met a girl I fancied as much as you

SOPHIE. Shut up Bernd

DR. SCHLESSINGER. No let me tell you

I've a fancy to give up my practice and carry this girl off to a place where we could go native she'd hunt for game and I'd roast it

Somewhere far away near the Amazon

M. AUZANNEAU. It's like we never existed except to cough up when she comes collecting for her birthday

MME. AUZANNEAU. Aren't they all like that these days?

M. AUZANNEAU. Never a word of thanks no gratitude

CANCÉ. Monstrous

The influence of a family whose chief aim was to come out on top

Choke any sign of affection and then you can savour your success such was the appalling upbringing yes monstrous the Prosecutor found the right word inflicted on this girl who was encouraged to be proud and arrogant

A murderess yes Members of the Jury but a victim as well a victim not a torturer unless it be to torture herself

The psychiatrists who were rather hastily discounted by
the Prosecutor are may I remind you experts you chose
for yourself

If you made a bad choice why don't you dismiss them?
You usually have faith in them don't you?

It just seems

That in this case you ignore anything you find embar-
rassing

You ignore everything that might tend to demolish your
theory of premeditation

A highly improbable theory but gifted as we know you
are you make up for your failure to prove it by pursu-
ing it with a ruthlessness which in all my career I have
rarely witnessed before

One of the three shots fired was at zero range and you
thought fit to label it the *coup de grâce* the death-blow
it's so easy to say but

How was it fired?

Suddenly as his body crumpled it must have fallen
against her and set the revolver off and this turns out to
be your *coup de grâce* a set of facts can be interpreted
in any way you like

CLAUDETTE. There are so many crossed lines Monsieur
le Président I'm not sure that there wasn't a time when
he was still in love with her and she had started to love
him

We all went to Antwerp once the three of us together to
visit a museum

CANCÉ. If after the attempt to take her life last month my
client was able to write "I believe there's a curse on my
family and on me as well" if she was able to understand that the time had come to make a confession

(The Fine Art Museum in Antwerp.)

SOPHIE. Look at that character

XAVIER. Which one?

SOPHIE. Leaning out of the window the sporty-looking type with something on his mind up there in the right-hand corner I like that picture

He looks like you.

XAVIER. And the girl with the red scarf on the other side of the road who seems to be gazing at him she looks like you

CANCÉ. If she was able to write "I hope Monsieur and Madame Bergeret can forgive me and take pity on my mother" doesn't this suggest she realised the time had come for her to redeem herself? So on her behalf

And with her own words

I ask you to forgive a girl whose real sin was pride

SOPHIE. She's horrible

XAVIER. I think she's not bad

SOPHIE. Are you serious?

XAVIER. If I met her in the street

SOPHIE. With that green nose and her yellow hands

I never realised

XAVIER. I'd follow her

SOPHIE. And I'd go for the sporty young raver with something on his mind I don't think the girl has treated him all that well look you can see she's going to eat her heart out

CANCÉ. And I believe I can ask you to forgive all those parents who think they know how to bring up their children and who make them into a replica of themselves living cheek by jowl with them without learning

to know them at all I ask you to forgive the manner in
which she defended herself and the blunders she made

SOPHIE. I wonder if the painter let the red paint run
down the canvas on purpose

It looks as if her heart's been bleeding

I never realised

CANCÉ. Forgive her too for having chosen to defend her
A feeble servant of the law

Who if he refuses to give way to tears can only appeal
to you with all the dignity he can muster

CLAUDETTE. You're taking your time

SOPHIE. Come and see and tell us if you think

If those two got together

It could lead to anything?

CLAUDETTE. It's an enormous picture

SOPHIE. Who painted it?

XAVIER. James Ensor

RECORDED VOICE. Sentences Sophie Auzanneau to
penal servitude for life

END